D. NUNEZ

FOOTBALL AND LIFE

Inside the World of True Fans

By Pitt Anddy

© Copyright 2024 - All rights reserved.

No part of this book may be copied, reproduced, or transmitted without express written consent from the publisher or the author. There shall be no legal or moral liability placed on the publisher or author for any losses, liabilities, or financial harm resulting directly or indirectly from the material in this book. You are in charge of your own decisions, deeds, and outcomes.

Legal Disclaimer: This book is copyrighted. This book is strictly for personal use only. Without the author's or publisher's permission, you may not change, distribute, sell, use, quote, or paraphrase any of the content in this book.

Disclaimer Notice: Please note the information contained within this document is for educational and entertainment purposes only. All effort has been executed to present accurate, up to date, and reliable, complete information. No warranties of any kind are declared or implied. Readers acknowledge that the author is not engaging in the rendering of legal, financial, medical, or professional advice.

The content within this book has been derived from various sources. Please consulta licensed professional before attempting any techniques outlined in this book. By reading this document, the reader agrees that under no circumstances is the author responsible for any losses, direct or indirect, which are incurred as a result of the use of the information contained within this document, including, but not limited to, errors, omissions, or inaccuracies.

INTRODUCTION

"D. Nunez – Football And Life" is an enthralling exploration into the life and achievements of Darwin Nunez, the celebrated Uruguayan football star. This meticulously crafted book delves deep into the less known aspects of Nunez's life, offering readers an array of untold stories, intriguing anecdotes, and hidden facts about his remarkable journey in the world of football.

From his early beginnings in Uruguay to his meteoric rise in Europe's premier football leagues, the book paints a comprehensive picture of Nunez's career. It is enriched with exclusive interviews, striking photographs, and thorough analyses, providing a comprehensive view of his life both on and off the pitch.

The book is not just a mere biography; it's a tribute to Nunez's skill, determination, and the enduring spirit that has won him accolades and admirers globally. It narrates the untold stories behind his successes, the resilience in the face of challenges, and the goals that fuel his ambition in the sport.

"D. Nunez – Football And Life" is an essential read for fans of Darwin Nunez and lovers of football alike, offering an immersive journey into the life of one of the sport's most promising talents. It's a celebration of his journey, highlighting the talent and passion that make him a standout figure in football.

HOW TO USE AUGMENTED REALITY (AR) TECHNOLOGY IN THIS BOOK

SCAN QR CODE

STEP 1 – Open camera & scan the QR code (No need to install any apps)

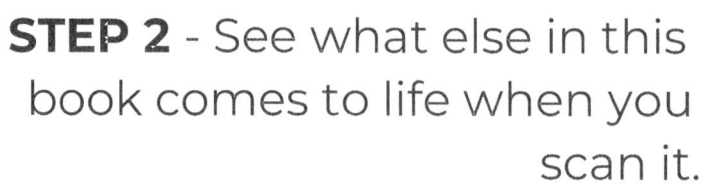

ACCESS AR PAGE

STEP 2 - See what else in this book comes to life when you scan it.

TABLE OF CONTENTS

INTRODUCTION 4

PERSONAL LIFE 9

CLUB CAREER 18

NATIONAL TEAM CAREER 26

RECORDS AND PERSONAL ACHIEVEMENTS 35

TECHNIQUE AND PLAYING STYLE 39

DO YOU WANT TO MEET DARWIN NUNEZ IN YOUR OWN SPACE?

Please scan the **QR code** to experience the **augmented reality (AR)** technology integrated into this book.

PERSONAL LIFE

- Early Struggles: Núñez grew up in a poor neighbourhood in Uruguay, learning the importance of sharing from a young age.
- School and Training: As a child, he attended school primarily for the meals provided and would head straight to football training afterwards.

- ⚽   Family Sacrifice: His brother, Junior, gave up his own football career at Peñarol to support their family, enabling Darwin to continue playing.
- ⚽   First Club: Núñez was initially signed by Peñarol at the age of 14 after impressing a scout.
- ⚽   Homesickness: He experienced homesickness after moving to Montevideo

and returned to his family for a year before rejoining Peñarol.

- ⚽ Early Talent Recognition: José Perdomo, a Uruguayan football legend, discovered Núñez at his academy in Artigas, leading to his move to Peñarol.
- ⚽ Injuries and Setbacks: Núñez suffered a significant knee injury early in his career,

requiring surgery and rehabilitation.

- ⚽ Move to Europe: He signed with Spanish club Almeria in 2019 for $4.5 million plus additional variables.
- ⚽ Success at Benfica: Núñez joined Benfica in 2020, winning Primeira Liga Player of the Year in 2021-22.
- ⚽ Liverpool Transfer: In 2022, he signed for Liverpool for a transfer fee that could reach

€100 million, making him the club's most expensive signing.

- ⚽ International Debut: Núñez made his debut for the Uruguayan national team in 2019 in a match against Peru, scoring his first international goal within minutes of coming on.
- ⚽ Personal Life: He has a child named Darwin with his partner Lorena Manas, who

he has been in a relationship with since 2020.

- ⚽ Tattoo Tribute: Núñez has a tattoo of his son, to which he points when celebrating goals.
- ⚽ Family-oriented: Despite his success, Núñez remains closely connected to his family and roots.
- ⚽ Physical Fitness: He maintains a rigorous fitness regime, even involving his

children in his workouts at home.

- ⚽ Love for the Sea: Núñez enjoys spending time at the beach and engaging in water sports like jet skiing.
- ⚽ Social Media Presence: He is active on social media platforms like Instagram and Twitter.
- ⚽ Net Worth: While his exact net worth is not publicly disclosed, his successful

football career, especially his record signing with Liverpool, suggests significant earnings.

⚽   Community Ties: He often reminisces about his humble beginnings and the communal spirit of his childhood neighborhood.

⚽   Coping with Challenges: Núñez has had to seek psychological help in the past due to the pressures of social media criticism during his career.

CLUB CAREER

- Early Start: Núñez started his football journey with the Uruguayan club Peñarol at 14.
- Initial Struggle: After joining Peñarol, Núñez felt homesick and returned to his previous club San Miguel de Artigas for a year.
- Injury Setback: He suffered a cruciate ligament injury early in his career, which required surgery.

- ⚽ Club Debut: Núñez made his debut in the first division of Uruguayan football at the age of 18.
- ⚽ Move to Europe: He was signed by Spanish club Almeria in 2019, scoring 16 goals in 30 appearances.
- ⚽ Record Transfer to Benfica: In 2020, Núñez joined Benfica for a club record fee of €24 million.

⚽   **Impressive Start at Benfica:** He scored a hat-trick in his first Europa League game for Benfica against Lech Poznań.

⚽   **Top Scorer in Primeira Liga:** Núñez was the top goal scorer in the Primeira Liga with Benfica in the 2021-22 season.

⚽   **Liverpool's Record Signing:** In 2022, he joined Liverpool for an initial fee of

£64 million, potentially rising to £85 million, making him the club's most expensive signing.

- ⚽ Champions League Impact: He became Benfica's top scorer in modern Champions League history, surpassing Nuno Gomes.
- ⚽ Interest from Other Clubs: Before joining Benfica, he attracted interest from clubs

like Brighton, Southampton, RB Leipzig, and Napoli.

⚽   Adaptation Challenges: Núñez struggled with the effects of COVID-19 and injuries during his time at Benfica.

⚽   Exceptional Goal-Scoring Rate: He led all forwards across Europe's top leagues in goals per 90 minutes in the 2021-22 season.

⚽   Clinical Finishing: Núñez had one of the highest non-penalty goal conversion rates in Europe in the 2021-22 season.

⚽   Sharp Shooter: He was known for his frequent shooting, averaging over three shots per game.

⚽   Versatile Forward: Núñez plays primarily as a centre forward but can also operate on the left side of the attack.

- ⚽ Champions League Experience: He gained valuable experience in the Champions League with Benfica.
- ⚽ Liverpool's Future Prospect: Jurgen Klopp signed him to bolster Liverpool's attack following Sadio Mane's departure.
- ⚽ Young Talent: He was signed by Liverpool at the age

of 23, showing his potential for future development.

- ⚽ Influential Performances: His performances in the Champions League against Liverpool were particularly influential in his signing by the club.

NATIONAL TEAM CAREER

- ⚽ Youth Levels: Darwin Nunez represented Uruguay in various youth national teams before making his senior team debut.
- ⚽ Senior Debut: Nunez made his debut for the senior Uruguayan national team in September 2020, showcasing

his rapid rise through the ranks.

- 2022 FIFA World Cup Qualifiers: He played a crucial role in Uruguay's 2022 FIFA World Cup qualifying campaign, contributing with goals and assists.
- World Cup Call-up: Nunez earned a spot in Uruguay's squad for the 2022 FIFA World Cup, marking a

significant achievement in his career.

- ⚽ International Goals: He scored his first goal for the senior national team shortly after his debut, highlighting his goal-scoring prowess.
- ⚽ Strike Partnership: Nunez formed a striking partnership with experienced forwards like Edinson Cavani and Luis Suarez in the national team setup.

- ⚽ Copa America Participation: He represented Uruguay in the 2021 Copa America, where the team reached the quarter-finals.
- ⚽ Young Talents: Nunez was part of a new generation of young talents emerging in the Uruguayan national team, bringing fresh energy and skills.
- ⚽ Scoring Against Strong Opponents: He demonstrated

his ability to score against strong international teams, earning respect as a formidable striker.

- ⚽ Versatility: Nunez's versatility allowed him to adapt to different tactical setups employed by the national team coach.
- ⚽ Coach's Trust: Coaches trusted Nunez to lead the line and be a focal point of the team's attack.

- ⚽ Continued Development: His national team experience provided a platform for continued development as a player.
- ⚽ International Friendlies: Nunez participated in international friendlies, gaining valuable experience against various opponents.
- ⚽ Competing in CONMEBOL: Competing in the competitive CONMEBOL

region exposed Nunez to high-intensity matches against top South American teams.

⚽   Part of the Goal-Scoring Squad: He was part of Uruguay's squad known for its attacking prowess and goal-scoring abilities.

⚽   World Cup Aspirations: Nunez's performances contributed to Uruguay's ambitions of securing a spot in the 2022 FIFA World Cup.

⚽   **Interactions with Legends:** Playing alongside legendary Uruguayan forwards like Cavani and Suarez provided Nunez with a unique learning experience.

⚽   **Fan Appreciation:** Nunez's performances earned him admiration from Uruguayan fans, who saw him as a promising talent.

- ⚽ Competition for Places: The national team competition for forward positions pushed Nunez to improve and excel.
- ⚽ Future Star: Nunez was widely regarded as one of Uruguay's future stars, with the potential to become a prominent figure in the national team's setup.

RECORDS AND PERSONAL ACHIEVEMENTS

⚽ Top Goal Scorer (2021/22): Darwin Núñez was the top goal scorer in Liga Bwin, netting an impressive 26 goals.

⚽ Player of the Year (2021/22): He was named the Player of the Year at SL Benfica, highlighting his exceptional performance during the season.

- ⚽ TM-Player of the Season (2022): Núñez earned the title of TM-Player of the Season in 2022.
- ⚽ English Super Cup Winner (2023): He was part of the Liverpool FC team that won the English Super Cup in 2023.
- ⚽ Uruguayan Champion Twice: Núñez won the

Uruguayan championship twice with CA Peñarol in the 2017/18 and 2016/17 seasons.

- ⚽ World Cup Participant (2022): He represented Uruguay in the 2022 World Cup.
- ⚽ Striker of the Year (2021/22): At SL Benfica, he was named Striker of the Year for the 2021/22 season.
- ⚽ Under-20 World Cup Participant (2019): Núñez

participated in the Under-20 World Cup in 2019 with Uruguay U20.

- ⚽ Significant Transfer Value: As of December 19, 2023, Darwin Núñez's market value was estimated at €65.00 million.
- ⚽ International Career: He has earned 22 caps and scored 8 goals for the Uruguay national team.

TECHNIQUE AND PLAYING STYLE

⚽ Physical Profile: Núñez is known for his athletic frame, which includes an upright posture, defined shape, and rangy length, making him a distinctive figure on the pitch.

⚽ Speed and Strength: His style is characterized by excellent acceleration and top speed, complemented by his strength, making him tough to stop once he gains momentum.

- ⚽ Versatility in Attack: He has shown versatility in attacking roles, effectively playing on the left flank in the Primeira Liga, where he uses his power and pace to dominate, and centrally in the Europa League, focusing more on linking up play and getting into the box.

- Goal Scoring: Núñez's goal-scoring ability is particularly prominent, with a notable goal every 68 minutes in the Europa League, compared to every 398 minutes in the Primeira Liga.
- Intelligent Movement: He is adept at making intelligent runs, especially between defenders, and utilizes his

body well in the box to create scoring opportunities.

- ⚽ Technical Skills: Despite having a limited technical skillset, Núñez adapts his game effectively, using his physical attributes to compensate.
- ⚽ Dribbling Style: His dribbling relies more on power and speed rather than intricate skill, making him

particularly effective in counter-attacking situations.

⚽ Innovative Play: He often drifts wide to act as a creator, using his intuition to create chances for teammates, including 30 chances and four assists in the Primeira League in one season.

⚽ Adapting to Challenges: While he sometimes struggles with consistency in touch, his intelligence in linking play and his goal-scoring prowess make up for it.

- Relentless Energy: A hallmark of Núñez's style is his relentless energy and tenacity, both in and out of possession, making him a persistent challenge for opponents.

Printed in Great Britain
by Amazon